*To my loves, Robert, April, and Richard:
You have taught me so much about embracing
the creative spirit and belief in oneself!*
—G. O. S.

To my mother, for always being the best teacher.
—A. L.

This is a work of fiction. Names, characters, places, and incidents either are the product of the author's imagination or are used fictitiously. Any resemblance to actual persons, living or dead, events, or locales is entirely coincidental.

Amazing Teachers & YOU!
Text Copyright © 2021 by Geraldine V. Oades-Sese
Illustrations Copyright © 2021 by Arthur Lin

All rights reserved. No part of this book may be reproduced or used in any manner without written permission of the copyright owner except for the use of quotations in a book review. For more information, address: DrGerry@childresilience.com.

First Edition, April 2021

Book design by Elynn Cohen

ISBN 978-1-7370619-0-8 (paperback)
ISBN 978-1-7370619-1-5 (hardcover)
ISBN 978-1-7370619-2-2 (ebook)

www.childresilience.com

AMAZING Teachers & YOU!

Geraldine V. Oades-Sese, PH.D.

illustrated by Arthur Lin

Teachers are amazing people.
They nurture your mind and guide your way,

Walk by your side and **inspire!**

Teachers can turn the ordinary into the **extraordinary**.

They help you travel to faraway lands, tread among the **dinosaurs**,

And remember...

Pause and take a deep breath,
Your teacher is there for you.
Tell them how you feel and why,
And they will help you through.

Teachers encourage you to **imagine and create**. They drive you to invent a flying school, pretend to sail the seven seas,

Erect a puppet theater and paint an original masterpiece!

Teachers show you how to **build and measure**. They challenge you to climb the highest hills, raise the tallest buildings, construct the strongest bridges

and race to **outer space**.

And remember...

Pause and take a deep breath,
Your teacher is there for you.
Tell them how you feel and why,
And they will help you through.

They push you to **tame** that angry lion,
surf a tidal wave,
Lift a gazillion pound weight and **face** those scary monsters!

But when you feel **frustrated**
or overwhelmed, don't hit or shout!

Instead, speak **softly** and **calmly.**
Use **kind words** and **gentle hands.**

And when your feelings become too big to handle, be **BRAVE** and **ASK for HELP**!

And remember...

Pause and take a deep breath,
Your teacher is there for you.
Tell them how you feel and why,
And they will help you through.

One day, you will remember those **amazing teachers**—
And how they nurtured and guided you!

Someday it will be **your turn** to share important lessons and inspire someone, too!

www.ingramcontent.com/pod-product-compliance
Lightning Source LLC
Chambersburg PA
CBHW041703160426
43209CB00017B/1731